Cooking With Words

Also by Diane Wahlheim and published by Ginninderra Press
Rhyme On My Mind (Picaro Poets)

Diane Wahlheim

Cooking With Words

Acknowledgements

'On Seeing a Young Man Smile' appeared in a different form in *Twilight Musings*, 2005

Thanks

To my long-time friend Harvey Collins for the illustrations at the start of each section

To the Ochre Coast Poets for their suggestions and critiques

To the Aldinga Beach University of the Third Age creative writers for their ideas and support

Cooking With Words
ISBN 978 1 76109 694 5
Copyright © text Diane Wahlheim 2024
Cover image: Diane Wahlheim

First published 2024 by
Ginninderra Press
PO Box 3461 Port Adelaide 5015
www.ginninderrapress.com.au

Contents

Foreword	9
Starters	
Cooking With Words	15
Lost and Found	17
Mistaken Identity	19
Switched On	20
Fatal Addiction	22
On Being a Senior	24
Thief	26
Reality	28
Show Stopper	29
Magic in His Name	31
Trade-off	32
No Longer in Service	34
It's Time	36
Sorting	37
When All Else Fails	38
Entrées	
Woe is Me	43
Copycat	45
Lollipop Man	46
Magpie	47
Reflections	48
Connected	49
Where's Fred?	50
Vision Splendid	51
Making Jam	52
Travelling	53
My Precious One	55

Unfair Dismissal	56
Looks of Love	58
A Spicy Tale	59
Cat's Whiskers	61
Reluctant Choice	62
Help!	64
If I Were Resurrected	65

Mains

Wander Through a Graveyard	69
The Man in the Wide-brimmed Hat	70
On Seeing a Young Man Smile	72
Strength	73
Watcher in the Night	74
What if?	75
It's Over	76
Ruckus in Aisle 3	77
Regret	78
Goodbye	80
Remember Me	81
Moments	82

Sweets

Surprise!	85
Never Too Old	87
Love Takes Courage	88
Shot in the Dark	90
Strike Breaker	92
DIY and a Husband Too	94
Dressing Room Danger	96
Hair Raising	98
Eye Opener	100
Missing in Action	102

Coffee and Conversation	103
The Big Question	105
Faith Can Move Mountains	106
A Letter from Mum	108
The Choice	109

Foreword

Diane Wahlheim has had a love affair with food and poetry for most of her life. As a young child living in Adelaide, she engaged in all things culinary via her mother, who was an exceptional home cook, and her father, who often took the reins at family barbecues. Also during those early years, Diane amused herself by writing 'ditties and rhymes', with the aid of a poetry book she had at home.

She was fortunate to have a primary school class teacher who encouraged poetry writing during English lessons. Diane recalls scribbling a poem when she was aged eight, with some students dubious she'd completed the task without help. So, after writing the first line of a ditty on the blackboard, her teacher then asked Diane to complete four lines in front of the class, which she accomplished easily to prove a point to any doubters.

Her good fortune in educators continued when a teacher in high school, an ardent poetry fan, brought works of Shakespeare, and particularly John Keats (Diane's favourite poet), to life. Diane also recalls listening at home to tunes from musicals, where many end words rhymed, and she remembers, as a young child, reciting small poems to her grandparents.

A brief hiatus in Diane's affair with food and poetry transpired when she became the switchboard operator and later the housekeeper at a retirement village in Adelaide. Her roles included managing the catering and general housekeeping staff. However, she still found time, on occasions, to pen poems about the village's employees.

She later resumed her passion for food when she became

co-owner of the Cherry Tree Cake Shop, in Birdwood, for four years, before surprising herself by winning a coveted cooking position at SA Government House, where she also wrote humorous rhymes for the in-house magazine. She became head cook at Government House and eventually stayed on for twenty-six years, feeding many governors and ambassadors, and royals such as Queen Elizabeth II and Prince Phillip, and Princess Diana and the then Prince Charles.

Diane retired to Aldinga Beach in 2013. It was time to focus more fully on poetry, and she joined the Ochre Coast Poets group in 2014. Diane's entertaining poems have won her many fans – she sold almost two hundred copies of her first short collection (or chapbook), *A Rhyme On My Mind*. 'I've always liked listening to and writing poems that made me and other people laugh,' Diane says. 'I love to be entertained.'

This first full collection of poetry will delight Diane's supporters. Sectionalised into four segments, each of which initially doffs a hat to her cooking background, the poems are varied and spiced with good humour.

The first section, appropriately entitled 'Starters', contains poems with a mostly solitary slant. She starts the collection with a signature poem which references her love of cooking – though with words now, rather than ingredients. Her delicious wit is reflected in most of the poems in this section.

The second section, 'Entrées', contains poems that are otherworldly, with a focus on objects and especially animals, particularly cats and dogs, which Diane idolises. Poems are a mix of rhyming and free verse.

Diane reveals her versatility by providing, in the third section, 'Mains', mostly unrhymed stanzas that are more serious.

Some poems border on enigmatic, while others are uncharacteristically solemn.

Diane returns to her forte of cracking hilarity in the final section, 'Sweets'. These poems, mainly concocted about pairs of people, are bound to be loved as she twists us around her little fingers with mirth, and has us hooked with rhyming bellyfuls of banter, as is her usual wont.

It has been a privilege to be involved in a small way to aid Diane in taking this journey. It felt often as if I was a secret passenger, tucked away in a suitcase jam-packed with chuckles.

Diane is eternally grateful to her two English teachers who provided the mentorship needed at an early age to help her to bring mirth into our lives. And, it's likely Mr Keats, should he somehow be bestowed a copy of *Cooking With Words* in the silence of his surrounds, would send out guffaws of giggles which would surely prompt those of us still of this world to be fondly tickled by her nibbles of unique humour.

Virgil Goncalves

Starters

Solo: Something undertaken or done alone; single-handed

Cooking With Words

My working days for many years
were a culinary delight.
I tested every recipe
to make sure I got it right.

My very favourite recipes
I still like to cook today.
The passion that I have for food
has never passed away.

Curries full of warming spice,
sizzling steak with black bean sauce,
or a degustation menu
that brings joy with every course.

Roasted lamb and steamed jam pudding,
apple pie with sweetened cream,
or hot scones dripping with butter
are all a foodie's dream.

Chocolate cake is still a favourite,
layered with cream and cherries,
and pavlova, crisp and crunchy,
topped with fat and juicy berries.

So many words entice us
and draw us to the plate –
the sweet, the sour and salty words,
and the spicy. They're all great.

But here in my retirement years,
though I really like to cook,
I am on a different path now –
cooking with words for my new book.

Lost and Found

I've lost my teef, he called out loud.
Where is the lost and found?
I sneezed, and out my mouth they flew,
then headed for the ground.
I simply must retrieve them
because they're my brand-new pair.
If I had an extra set at home
I wouldn't really care,
but I can't chew my steak without them
and I haven't got a spare.

The assistant at the counter
was listening with intent
to the quite distraught complainant,
and asked where he'd thought they went.
If I knew that, love, I'd tell you,
and they'd be back in my mouth.
All I know is, when I sneezed,
the choppers headed south.

Where were you when it happened?
She was trying not to laugh.
I was over in the spices aisle,
buying crystals for my bath.
Someone dropped a thing of pepper –
it flew high into the air.
The pepper landed everywhere,
even got some in my hair.

So I moved towards the freezer aisle,
away from pepper dust,
but then the sneezing started,
geez I thought that I would bust.
The assistant did her very best
to help him with his claim.
I'll put a call out in the store –
we'll find your teeth again.

She got on to the store PA.
We need a clean-up in aisle nine
and if anybody sees some teeth…
He interjected, They are mine!
She got a very quick response,
from Tom in the freezer aisle.
He said, I think I've found them –
I've got a salmon with a smile.

Mistaken Identity

He had to spend a night in jail.
I am innocent, said he.
I really didn't do this crime!
But we caught you on TV.

You robbed a bank at gun-point,
put the money in a sack,
then set off down the alley
without even looking back.

You jumped a six-foot iron fence,
raced across the nearby park,
then climbed a tree and waited
until it was really dark.

I tell you that guy isn't me –
you have made a huge mistake.
I don't care what your TV shows.
Just listen, for goodness sake.

I never held up any bank
and I've never owned a gun.
Also, with a wooden leg,
I simply cannot run.

The guy you want is still out there.
Can't you see it isn't me?
And to run and jump a six-foot fence
isn't easy at ninety-three.

Switched On

He had signed up for a dance class
thinking dancing would be nice.
But it proved to be expensive –
he could not afford the price.

He had hoped to win the lotto,
but that hadn't come to pass.
So how could he find the money
to pay for the dancing class?

Then he had a flash of insight.
It came to him from the blue.
I'll become a male escort,
yes, that's just what I will do.

So he got a big makeover
of his body, hair and face.
He pressed his suit and shone his shoes,
there was nothing out of place.

He was really quite successful
in his chosen new career,
and, in no time, he was voted
the male escort of the year.

He became so very busy,
there was no time for himself.
His dancing shoes, no longer used,
gathered dust upon the shelf.

When he finally retired,
he was too worn out to dance.
So now he just wears ugg boots,
and some comfy trackie pants.

Fatal Addiction

Daryl just loved mushrooms,
they were his breakfast, lunch and tea.
Any food containing mushrooms
was the perfect food, said he.

He made them into mushroom soup,
pasta and risotto, too.
He ate them fried on wholewheat toast,
even made them into stew.

He loved the dried porcini ones,
he said their flavour was immense.
He kept them in a big glass jar
for his mushroom food events.

His parties were amazing,
menus long with haute cuisine.
Friends loved to be invited,
'twas the best food ever seen.

He had cook books on his bookshelf
that were filled with recipes
of how to cook up mushrooms,
and he tackled those with ease.

His great knowledge of the fungi
was known all around the town.
There was no one who knew more
than mushroom lover Daryl Brown.

But alas, poor Daryl cooks no more
for he made a sad mistake.
When he fried up poisoned mushrooms,
it caused such a belly ache.

Now Daryl Brown lies underground,
it's a sorry tale but true.
He's buried underneath the trees
where his poisoned mushrooms grew.

On Being a Senior

I could say that life from here on in
may wear our nerves a little thin.
Things go missing, memory fades,
your car keys hide, as do your shades.
But I won't say that.

I could say now the little things,
like a phone that rings and rings and rings,
or a blackbird's call that wakes you up
when you've only managed your eyes to shut,
will drive you mad.
But I won't say that.

I could say that it's all downhill –
you'll be moving while you're standing still.
You might forget just where you are
and God knows where you left the car.
But I won't say that.

What I will say is it's time for fun.
You can walk or shuffle if you cannot run.
No one can tell you what to do,
just please yourself. It's what I do.

Life's there to live, so shake its tail,
rattle its cage and make it wail.
Enjoy yourself, you've earned the right
to party on into the night.

So when someone who's only fifty
says, For your age you look quite nifty,
just wink and smile and keep them guessing.
You're still kicking, and that's a blessing.

Thief

She was sitting by the river
It was such a lovely day
The sun was warm, the breeze was soft.
It was perfect in every way.

Until…
Help, stop that thief. He's got my bag!

She looked up to see a runner
coming straight to where she sat.
His head was bent and covered
by a funny, floppy hat.

It was plain he wasn't looking
so she knew she must be quick.
As he reached where she was sitting,
she just put out her stick.
It tripped him up, and down he went
and on his face fell flat.
Then as he tried to find his feet,
she gave his head a whack.

He yelled in pain, but once again,
tried getting to his feet.
So she poked him in the stomach
while staying in her seat.
It was then he lost his balance
and went rolling down the bank.
He rolled into the water
and very quickly sank.

A crowd began to gather,
quite amazed at what they saw.
The police got in and pulled him out
while he screamed at her and swore.
That silly old bat attacked me,
my head is cut and sore.
Old, I'm not old, she said,
I'm only eighty-four.

The stolen bag had been returned,
the stick was by her side.
As the grateful woman thanked her,
she felt a little pride.
The police said she was very brave
as they hauled the thief away.
Not brave – I just didn't want his kind
to spoil my perfect day.

Reality

What about reality
that isn't really real?
The shows that flood our living rooms,
how do they make us feel?
There doesn't seem to be a thing
worth watching on the box.
Do they put the writers in a room
and make sure the door is locked?

And yet reviews are really good
for this awful, dreary stuff.
We should switch it off, we really should,
it is just not good enough.
But woe is me, in the year ahead,
it will all be back again.
So searching for a decent show
will be futile and in vain.

There'll be people in the jungle,
there'll be bachelors on the prowl.
Cooking shows and building shows,
and shows that make you scowl.
I'm going to turn the telly off
and join a good book club.
Forget about reality,
I'm going down the pub.

Show Stopper

The make-up was perfection
on every actor's face.
The musicians all were ready,
the conductor took his place.

The audience was seated
and ready for the show,
but the tenor was in trouble,
for little did they know,
he'd tripped on the extension lead
and his head took quite a blow.

He slid clumsily across the stage,
face first into the floor,
poor man he was quite injured
and the blood began to pour.

The audience was so upset
to see the sorry sight
but when he finally found his feet,
they really got a fright.
His mouth was bruised and bloodied
and one eye was swollen shut.
He made a loud and mournful cry
that came right from his gut.

He fell again down to the floor,
his cry rose to the roof.
He held his hand above his head
and in it was a tooth.
He'd knocked it out when he fell down,
poor fellow was distressed.
They picked him up and took him off,
he was really in a mess.

The patrons in the higher seats,
on the third-tier balcony,
were using their binoculars
to enable them to see.

I'm not quite sure what's going on,
said someone from the top.
It must be something serious
that's caused the show to stop.
Eventually, the stage was clean
and the actors back in place
but the tenor's night was ruined
and, alas, so was his face.

So, if you're going to a show,
please just remember this:
if you don't take your binoculars,
who knows what you might miss.

Magic in His Name

Michael was a handsome boy.
He was tall and dark with muscles.
He was strong and known to always win
the schoolyard scuffles and tussles.

He went to university,
thought he'd be an engineer.
But a life upon the acting stage
was where he wanted a career.

He ditched his course and off he went
to learn to dance and sing.
A casting agent spied him
and said, I've got the very thing.

There is a group of handsome men
that puts a show on every night.
They're looking for an extra guy
and I think you'll be just right.

Your dancing is perfection
and you'll soon learn the routine.
Boy, when you take your clothes off,
you will make the women scream.

So Michael was an instant hit,
they had never seen his like.
He became the star of every show
and was known as Magic Mike.

Trade-off

The virus. This blessed virus,
it is with us every day.
The advice just keeps on coming –
how to keep this bug away.

We wash our hands, we stay inside.
We're so careful when we shop.
We have to do our very best
to help infections stop.

My hands have never been so clean,
my benches all wiped down.
My computer's into overdrive
with fun emails passed around.

I am cleaning out my cupboards.
I am sorting out my clothes.
When I get into the corners,
hidden treasures are exposed.

The things I haven't seen for years,
packed in boxes in the shed,
are suddenly revealed again.
Even books I've never read.

To say, I just can't find the time,
now simply isn't true.
With this sorting journey started,
I will have to see it through.

There'll be many cups of coffee,
homemade biscuits, cups of tea.
A glass or two of 'healthy' wine
to inspire and comfort me.

So while I am in lockdown
I'll resolve to do my part,
and I'll keep the red wine flowing,
cos it's so good for the heart.

No Longer in Service

Well, things have really changed now.
It's not like it was before.
I've not been left alone like this
since nineteen ninety-four.

I'm usually in her handbag.
It's my job to help her spend.
In fact, there have been shopping days
I thought would never end.

Now things are really not the same.
Her shopping's been curtailed.
For on one fatal shopping day,
she really was derailed.

There were so many packages,
she could barely lift them all.
She'd spent me well in every shop
as she wandered down the mall.

When, finally, we got back home,
there was very little space
to put the daily purchases.
It was simply a disgrace.

She opened up the cupboard
beneath the staircase in the hall,
but the parcels tightly packed in there
began to slip and fall.

She landed flat out on her back,
covered with parcels head to toe.
She ended up in hospital –
her recovery was slow.

So now I'm here, stuck in this drawer
and my life is not the same.
Those wild, exciting shopping days
may never come again.

How I dream of our adventures.
I hope one day I'll be free –
and released from this dark prison
to go on a shopping spree.

It's Time

Goodbye to several of the things I knew,
like high heels, now a flatter shoe.
Goodbye to late nights on the town,
coming home as the sun went down.
I think of all the years gone by,
years of my youth, I've watched them fly.

But now I'm glad to say hello
to new things and a life that's slow.
To have the time dear friends to see,
when they have time to spend with me.
I do not need to rush around,
a quieter pace I now have found.

But even though we say adieu
to things that we no longer do,
let's not forget what's gone before
and dip inside our memories' store.
Treasure what has brought us here
and hold our journey's memory dear.

Sorting

I am sitting and I'm sorting
for I'm told that we are moving.
All my old and worn-out toys will have to go!
But what to keep, and what to not
is so puzzling and confusing,
and the answer to it, I just do not know.

I am sitting and I'm sorting.
I see Teddy has some bruising.
He has lost an ear and one arm's hanging low.
But, as Teddy is my best friend,
I just know I can't include him
in the box Mum has marked Things To Throw.

I am sitting and I'm sorting.
How I wish I wasn't choosing.
All my friends should go with me – it's such a blow!
How can I go without them?
I will have to talk to Granny
cos there's something she is good at. She can sew!

We are sitting and we're mending,
and my Granny's really moving,
stitching ears and eyes and noses. She's not slow.
By the time that we are finished,
say 'round six o'clock or seven,
there won't be a single friend we have to throw!

When All Else Fails

My pile of books had really grown.
I no longer had the space.
So off I set to buy some shelves
to keep them all in place.

The bookshelf that I chose was fine.
It seemed sturdy, large and strong.
I thought it came assembled
but sadly, I was wrong.

The one you see is on display,
the salesman said to me.
You put the shelves together.
It's as easy as can be.

I looked the salesman in the eye.
I said, You're joking, right?
I have to build this thing myself?
I'll be up half the night.

The bookcase was delivered in
a great big cardboard box,
secured with plastic strappy things
as hard as granite rocks.

I opened up the flat pack,
tipped the contents on the floor.
There was wood and screws and other things
I'd never seen before.

The salesman said, It's easy as –
words that put me at my ease.
So I started to construct the shelves
thinking, This will be a breeze.

When I looked at my creation,
my smile turned to a frown.
The outside bits were all inside
and one panel upside down.

What had I done? This wasn't good.
I'd made a huge mistake.
I even had screws over,
and my legs began to shake.

The one thing I'd forgotten
was the small instruction book.
When all else fails, I said out loud,
I had better take a look.

At three a.m., I made some tea
and admired what I had done.
A sturdy bookcase stood there.
The challenge had been won.

So what's my very favourite book
sitting proudly on the shelf?
It's the one that gives instructions
to build a bookcase by myself.

Entrées

Otherworldly: Strange and wonderful, like something out of a story; unreal

Woe is Me

I dreamt I was Father Christmas.
The year was thirty, thirty-two.
I was having lots of problems
and not sure what I should do.

The reindeer now were very old,
many with arthritic pain,
and some of them could hardly walk
so would never fly again.

I couldn't just replace them,
magic reindeer are quite rare,
and even Aldi's special buys
had no flying reindeer there.

Then I thought that maybe Uber
could deliver the toys for sure,
but they went out of business
in twenty, twenty-four.

And the elves were so unhappy,
quite a few of them in tears.
They complained they'd had no pay rise
in more than a hundred years.

So how to fix these problems –
what action should I take?
Then suddenly to my delight,
I found myself awake.

So should you see Father Christmas
sitting in a Santa chair,
surrounded by a lot of kids,
you should know why he's there.

He's really not enjoying it,
no matter how he tries.
He's really there to get the cash
for Aldi's special buys.

Copycat

The cat lay in the morning sun,
he had no thought to jump or run.

No mouse to chase, no bird to prowl,
he made no sound, no murmured growl.

And as I watched the sleeping cat,
I thought we all should be like that.

With head and feet and tail tucked in,
block out the jarring, noisy din.

Forget the stress of every day
and sometimes sleep our cares away.

Lollipop Man

He stands on the road.
We obey his every direction.

Behind him
monstrous machines
growl and grind.

We sit and wait.
Patience wanes.

The lollipop man
holds us
in his power.

Just two commands:

SLOW
STOP

STOP
SLOW

He is in control.
We have no say.
We sit and wait.

The little boy on the footpath
grips his mother's hand,
eyes wide with wonder
at all the giant machines.

To him,
this is Disneyland.

Magpie

He woos me every morning
with a sweet and welcome song,
then patiently he sits and waits
hoping I won't take too long.

He watches me intently,
tilts his head so he can see.
I know he's only there for food
but that doesn't bother me.

Always dressed in black and white,
such a formal bird is he.
I watch him as he struts around,
an amusing sight to see.

Sometimes he calls to other birds
to join the daily fare.
Quite often they eat all the food
but he doesn't seem to care.

He could be a philanthropist
to each feathered creature friend,
but maybe he's just showing off.
Does his ego have no end?

Dear bird, you leave me smiling
as I go about my day,
and thank you for your visit,
as I watch you soar away.

Reflections

Mirror, mirror on the wall,
oh, what a mess if you should fall.

The glass might cut my fragile feet,
and blood could spill into the street.

The neighbourhood would be aghast
to hear the ambo's siren blast.

Oh, come on, mirror, can't you see
that it would be a tragedy?

If you should lose your fixture place,
I'd have nowhere to see my face.

I'm not sure why I worry so,
you've never made a move to go.

But work I've had to do at home,
makes you the subject of this poem.

A silly poem, oh yes, indeed,
just there for other folk to read.

So here we are at poem's end.
Thank God for that, my mirror friend.

Connected

He looks at me with deep brown eyes.

He doesn't speak.
No words needed,
not between us.

His eyes follow my every move.

I grab my coat.
Is it time for a walk?
He wags his tail.

I'm sure that's a smile.

Where's Fred?

Some lowlife stole my garden gnome.
They took him from his loving home
and now he's out there all alone.
It is really stressing me.

I named my little fellow, Fred.
The lawn on which he stood is dead.
I'd put a pot plant there instead
but it's Fred I want to see.

My little gnome is short and fat,
with a flowing beard and a pointed hat.
A blue waistcoat – I painted that.
Such a handsome gnome is he.

They took him in the dead of night.
He must have got an awful fright.
And nicking gnomes just isn't right.
Oh, wherever can he be?

So, if you're on a walk one day
and see my Freddy on display,
please contact me without delay.
I will pay a finder's fee.

Vision Splendid

Golden locks a splendorous veil,
falling down, encumbering you.
Standing there you look so frail,
awaiting winter's hand on you.

He'll strip you down of all your glory
and leave you cold and bare.

You seem to stand expectantly,
your head bowed as if you cry.
And yet your beauty captures me.
It lifts my heart and makes me sigh.

Oh willow, willow, autumn dressed,
lift up your head with pride.

Making Jam

It's summer and we're making jam.
There're apricots and cherries,
and big, fat plums we cut by hand,
plus all the summer berries.

The jam pan's from our Aunty Jill.
Its use is a tradition.
It's very old but going still –
and in such good condition.

The stove is on, the sugar's in,
sweet perfumes fill the room.
The kids are hanging out for when
it's time to lick the spoon.

It always was the summer plan
when we were all together.
With ripened fruit we cooked the jam,
no matter what the weather.

And now we're back and once again,
sweet fruit is in the pan.
There's lots to do. We don't complain.
It is summer – time for jam.

Travelling

I am going on a holiday.
I've been many times before,
and am all packed up and ready,
headed for a distant shore.

But as I am much older now,
I am careful not to fall,
because falling could undo me
and would not be good at all.

I could get bruised and battered,
spreadeagled on the ground,
and if my zipper should fly open
there'd be problems quite profound.

Got lost inside an airport once.
It gave me such a fright.
Wasn't quite sure how it happened –
I was nearly there all night.

I am frayed around the edges
and a little worse for wear,
but that doesn't mean I'm useless.
I just need a bit more care.

Now waiting here to be picked up,
a brand-new adventure waits.
The car is here and off we go,
heading for the airport gates.

Although I'm riding in the boot,
they say lovely things of me:
That old suitcase has served us well –
since nineteen eighty-three.

My Precious One

You fix your gaze on me with amber eyes.
Within your breast, there lies a cruel heart.
A feline soul that does not sympathise
that I'm just here to play a servant's part.

I gladly give you everything you need,
but is it fair that you give nothing back?
There seem to be no limits to your greed.
It's gratitude and thanks you seem to lack.

I watch you as you lie there in the sun.
You stretch and roll and yawn, then back to bed
while I, your slave, your every errand run.
You spend your day just waiting to be fed.

But woe is me. I love you, lazy cat.
Who knows, one day you just might love me back.

Unfair Dismissal

I'm sitting in the bottom drawer
and I'm really not amused.
I've led a very active life,
now I'm hardly ever used.

Then I guessed just how it happened,
this sudden fall from fame.
It was the kid with purple hair.
Yes, he's the one to blame.

He didn't hold me properly,
when I slipped, he cut his hand.
Then, he screamed, We need a new one,
all-electric would be grand.

So now I'm in this awful space.
It's not where I want to be.
It's full of things no longer used,
this is not the place for me.

My companions in the bottom drawer
are not really in my class.
There's a length of string, rubber bands,
and a piece of broken glass.

There's a ball of wool, some scissors,
a book from nineteen eighty-three.
Other things I'm not quite sure of
are all cuddled up with me.

There are plastic bits and pieces,
a rusty grater and a comb.
This is the worst I've ever felt
since my owners brought me home.

Will this be my life forever?
No! I'm sure I'll hear them say,
Where the hell's the old can opener?
There is no power today!

Looks of Love

I waited for you.
I knew you would come one day.

I watched you walk past.
Then, you turned.

I waited.
You looked at me.

I didn't have to do anything.
No tricks, no begging.

All I had to do
was look back at you.

Now, I am here,
tucked in my own bed.

Warm.
Wanted.
Loved.

You're in your chair,
watching me.

I rest my head on my paws
and give in to sleep.

A Spicy Tale

The cupboard folk were chatting
as they sat upon the shelves.
Just look at them, the mustard said,
they're so happy with themselves.

They are never in the cupboard
like the rest of us poor sods.
They act so damned important.
Who made them the spicy gods?

Well, they are the salt and pepper,
said the cinnamon out loud.
The family use them every day,
so I guess that makes them proud.

Well, for goodness sake, stop whinging,
said the cumin, finely ground.
When I fell out four years ago,
they put me back, the wrong way round.

I've still got my plastic wrap on
said paprika, with a scowl.
I don't know why they bought me,
I'm sure I'm not so spicy now.

And I came from their old house,
said dried sage, so don't complain.
They used me once in ninety-three
but I've not been out again.

Did you catch their act at breakfast?
said dried parsley flakes. I mean,
Why not use me? The scrambled eggs
are much better with some green.

So the spicy group decided
though it wasn't really right,
they would just have to accept it
as they'd never win the fight.

Salt and pepper were the victors
in the spicy preference games,
and it seemed that getting used up
depended upon your name.

Cat's Whiskers

A bumper sticker that made me laugh
said,
Dogs have masters. Cats have staff.

Well, I can say that this is true.
If you have a cat, you'll know it too.
I love my cat. Does he love me?
I guess he does, especially

the times when he wants out or in,
and I'm there to indulge his whim.
He curls up on my favourite chair,
no room for me. He doesn't care.

When friends drop in, that's when he starts
to slowly wash his private parts.
That's one fine cat, I hear them say.
Yes, one that I should give away.

But this cat's smart, I must admit.
For when I think I'll pack his kit,
he comes and jumps upon my knee
and purrs, and looks straight up at me.

And as I stroke his head and chin,
this feline seems to give a grin.
He settles down quite happily
to have a nap before his tea.

Reluctant Choice

I think the time has come for me
to just wear sensible shoes.
The ones that keep me steady, though
they are not the ones I'd choose.

Gone are the wild and heady days
of high heels and leather boots.
The days of fashion glamour,
haute couture and tailored suits.

There always was a shoe to match
whatever I chose to wear
and, if not, the solution was
to purchase a brand-new pair.

Now alas, I think that ageing
has dealt me this cruel blow.
When I've packed up my lovely heels,
to the op shop they will go.

I guess the upside of this is
back and knee strain won't be there.
And there'll no fear of falling
off a flat and boring pair.

I still can dress up to the nines
for a show or a dinner treat,
and I think I look amazing
till I look down at my feet.

The ugly shoes stare back at me –
they're the ones that I had to choose.
Like it or not, the time has come
to start wearing sensible shoes.

Help!

The carpet needs a shampoo.
It's as grotty as can be.
We have to get a guy to come
to remove the spots we see.

The dog has done a piddle
and it's left a nasty stain.
He squatted in the corner –
to clean it up will be a pain.

We will need a big, strong steamer
to help us with this task.
You'll never get that stain out,
said someone who wasn't asked.

We have to clean the carpet.
It really must be done.
So ring the carpet cleaning guy
cos the landlord's got a gun.

If I Were Resurrected

If, somehow, I returned again,
who would I like to be?
What about a famous poet?
Maybe Byron, Keats, Shelley.

I could sit in Café Greco,
drinking coffee with my mates.
We would write our poems on napkins
and have deep, intense debates.

And full of poetic passion,
write of life and death, and more.
We would not have fame and riches,
but not care that we were poor.

We would write our poems and sonnets,
odes to love and nature's gifts,
pay homage to joy and beauty,
things that make our spirits lift.

But.

If I returned, I'd still be me,
maybe write a small chapbook.
If I had known Keats or Shelley,
I'd have probably been their cook.

Mains

Pensive: Deep in thought; contemplative

Wander Through a Graveyard

While wandering through this quiet space,
I feel a gentle lifting breeze.
There are so many resting here,
beneath the tall and shady trees.

The headstones talk of loved ones lost,
long years ago. Some young, some old.
I wonder how those lives were lived
and were their stories ever told?

A magpie finds a place to sit,
and watches me as I pass by.
Am I intruding in this place?
He turns to me, a curious eye.

Now as I slowly move around,
I read of those who've gone before.
Some lives were lost right here at home
and some upon a distant shore.

The time has come for me to go.
The evening dew is coming down.
Before I leave this sacred place,
I take a final look around.

The gentle breeze moves through the trees
and as I turn to say goodbye,
the magpie lifts his head to sing
a warbled song to the sky.

The Man in the Wide-brimmed Hat

He really struck an awesome sight,
the man in the wide-brimmed hat.
He walked the streets when it was dark.
In his hand he held a cat.

People whispered in the village,
wondering just who he could be.
As he passed, they moved the curtains,
peering out so they could see.

He never stopped, he never spoke,
he just went about his day.
His head was bent to hide his face
but his hair was long and grey.

Then one day, he just disappeared.
The man in the wide-brimmed hat.
It was then the town discovered –
so had every single cat.

The townsfolk were disturbed and said,
Oh, whatever will we do?
Have we had a witch among us
and we didn't have a clue?

They gathered in the local hall.
They were worried and afraid,
but in spite of many questions
their fears were not allayed.

Though that was many years ago,
in the town there's still no cat.
And not a single person there
is game to wear a hat.

On Seeing a Young Man Smile

If I should walk a thousand miles
and, walking, see a thousand smiles,
I never will, not once, forget
that slightly upturned look and, yet,
although I know 'twas not for me,
I swear, for all eternity,
I'll say it was.

A gentle smile, just barely there
and yet, it filled the very air,
reminding me, when just a boy,
your heart so young and full of joy,
you turned your lovely face to me
and swore, for you, there'd never be
another love.

Strength

We knew this day would come.
There was plenty of warning.
Doctors, counsellors and such
painted the picture clearly.
While there was time and energy,
we did all the things she wanted to do.
We reached down to the deepest core
to where love was stored, to give her our all.
Yet now, as we stand here,
grief has overwhelmed us.
We realise, through it all,

it was she who was supporting us.

Watcher in the Night

He watches, in the dead of night,
the people of the tiny town.
The night is dark, no yellow moon,
there're only rabbits moving round.

The silent night holds memories close,
and yet the watcher, wide awake,
can see inside the sleepers' dreams,
and from their dreaming secrets take.

Who is this watcher standing there
who sees the dreamers in the night?
And will he keep their secrets safe
when morning sheds her warming light?

Now moving slowly through the dark,
the creatures of the village go,
across the silent, cobbled streets
to where the boats bob to and fro.

What if?

How I wish that I could see
what lies ahead for you and me.
I'd then avoid the things that harm
and concentrate on things that charm.

Alas, we can't the future see,
that is our reality.
So to reflect on what might be
is just a waste of time.

If I could just go back in time,
retrace my steps and change my mind,
would things alter or would I find
I'd do it all again?

It's Over

Here we are in the midst of strife.
We tried to keep the peace.
We tried to live a normal life
and not to render grief.

In spite of efforts strong and true,
our bonds became untied.
You ask me what I feel for you.
Well, I'm just feeling tired.

We seem to tear each other down
And bicker, stress and fight.
Is no solution to be found?
Is there no end in sight?

The flame's gone out, the passion's spent.
There's nothing left to give.
Let's stop it now and be content
to know it's time to leave.

Ruckus in Aisle 3

I can hear her long before I can see her.

I turn into the sweets aisle
and there she is,
lying prostrate on the floor –
a tear-stained, red-faced child.

The mother,
continuing with her shopping,
is somehow rendered deaf.

I steer my trolley
around the
banshee
and try to quell
thoughts of
murder
in my head.

At the checkout, I can still hear the screams.

I leave the shopping centre
and find I have forgotten the milk.
Shall I go back?

No.
Tomorrow will do.

Regret

I used to have a magic broom,
and I called him Hex Magor.
A really strong and sturdy broom,
made of hickory wood and straw.

My Hex's place was by the door
and no one ever knew
of all the magical, mystical things
that broom of mine could do.

I never was a wicked witch.
I just really liked to fly.
With Romulus, my blackest cat,
we'd ride Hexie through the sky.

But through the years I'd put on weight
so we could not carry on.
My broom stood idle by the door –
all our flying days were gone.

Hex seemed to lose the will to live.
His magic powers were slow.
He started shedding bits of straw.
It was time for him to go.

I gave him to a younger witch
who had just begun to fly –
perfect for someone starting out
to ride the evening sky.

My magic broom did very well.
His new owner was impressed.
His special powers were all renewed.
Among his peers, he was the best.

A hundred years have passed me by.
I still miss him every day.
I loved that broom and really wish
I'd not given him away.

Goodbye

When I was young you held my hand
and made sure that I was safe.
You let me have a daytime nap.
You washed my hands and face.

And now it's I who holds your hand,
making sure that you are safe.
I let you have a day-time nap
and I wash your hands and face.

Your love for me still brightly shines
as it has throughout the years.
And as I hold your fragile hand,
now's not the time for tears.

The time has come for you and me
to continue on our way.
As we travel on life's journey,
let's give thanks for every day.

Remember Me

Cry for me, but not for long.
Don't linger in sad shadows.
I would not want that for you.
Remember the happy times.

I stayed as long as I could.
But now I travel on alone.
You must continue, too.

Be kind to each other.
Show love and care.
Remember me.
I'll always be near.

Moments

Our days are filled with moments small
though we cannot recall them all.
To recognise them when they call
will lift us from the darkest fall.

An opening rose, a sheer delight,
a cactus flower that scents the night.

A child's sweet face, a secret look,
a symphony, a treasured book.

A kiss that takes us by surprise,
a hug that makes our senses rise.

Just sitting in a sunshine's beam
can give us time to think and dream.

Home-baked treats that fill us up
or drinking tea from a china cup.

The sound of laughter, strong and clear,
the beauty of a glistening tear.

To thank someone for being kind
just takes a fragment of our time.

So let's enjoy our moments small.
Be grateful that they're there at all.
For beautiful moments are a gift
and help nudge gloomy times adrift.

Sweets

Coupling: Act of bringing or coming together; pairing

Surprise!

He was very disappointed
and was really quite upset.
The family gave no greeting –
he never thought that they'd forget.

This was a special birthday,
a milestone in his life.
Yet, there were no birthday wishes,
not even from his wife.

He thought, I won't remind them
so he just set off for work.
But he wasn't very happy –
their lack of thought began to irk.

His secretary sensed his mood,
asking, What has made you frown?
Oh, I'm okay, he said to her,
it's just my family's let me down.

I'll take you out to lunch, she said,
that will brighten up your day.
He said, That will be very nice,
it will chase my blues away.

So they went out to a restaurant,
where the food was really fine.
They talked and ate and also drank
a lot of fine, red wine.

She said, Let's not go back to work,
I don't live far from here.
I could make us both some coffee
or I've got a nice, cold beer.

So he followed her to her place.
He did feel a little strange.
She said, Sit there on the sofa.
I won't be long – I'll just get changed.

The wine had really kicked in now.
He was calm and wasn't stressed.
Then he had a sudden impulse
to take his clothes off, so undressed.

Suddenly, the bedroom door
was opened with 'Surprise!'
He heard lots of cheery voices
and could not believe his eyes.

His entire family stood there,
holding a big cake in a box.
He stared at them in disbelief,
wearing nothing but his socks.

Never Too Old

Said he, My bones are aching.
What do you expect? she said.
You've spent hours in the garden.
Have a bath and go to bed.

Do you think that I am past it?
Past it? What do you mean?
You know, just old and useless
like a rusty, worn machine.

Okay, you aren't the sprightly lad
who swept me off my feet,
but you've always been my hero –
you are caring, kind and sweet.

You've kept every single promise
that you made when we were wed.
You've supported me and loved me,
and were always good in bed.

Have you been at the sherry?
he asked her with a wink.
No, to tell you that I love you
does not require a drink.

She took his hand and he took hers.
Then they wandered down the hall,
their walking sticks supporting them,
just in case they'd have a fall.

Love Takes Courage

From the very day he met her,
his world was blown apart.
She smiled at him and that was it,
Cupid's arrow hit his heart.

What's happened to him? said his friends.
He is like a different man.
He's gone all soft and giggly,
we just don't understand.

I think he's met a woman
and she's got him in a whirl.
Then someone said, I've seen her,
she's no woman, just a girl.

His mother won't be happy
when he tells her of his plan –
to run off and get married.
We know what will hit the fan!

We've seen how very brave he is,
when it comes to fighting crimes.
And he never shrinks from danger,
that is when his courage shines.

But dealing with his mother's
a completely different thing.
and he never has defied her,
though he's had the casual fling.

I wonder if he'll see it through.
Maybe then his mum will see
he has the strength to stand his ground
and finally break free.

Well, love is very strong, you know
so I'm sure there's room for hope.
I guess if things get nasty,
they've got the option to elope.

No, he doesn't stand a chance,
though he'd be a wondrous lover.
The fact is: he's not strong enough
to stand up to his mother.

Shot in the Dark

My Aunty Mae and Uncle Fred
owned a station quite remote.
While droving, Fred, away for months,
travelled far and never wrote.
And Aunt Mae was left to manage,
such a stoic soul was she.
Single-handed she ran the farm,
and was like a Mum to me.
Aunt Mae had always kept a gun,
just behind the kitchen door.
It was there for her protection –
that was what she used it for.
Dealing with the farming chores,
many trials she would face.
The drought, the snakes, and oftentimes
an intruder on the place.

One stormy night, she heard a noise.
Was that drifter back again?
She grabbed her gun, took aim and fired,
then she heard a scream of pain.
You have shot me, Mae, you've shot me.
It was the voice of Uncle Fred.
She rushed outside to take a look
and found uncle lying dead.
Not one person in the family
ever knew of Fred's demise.
Or how he had returned that night,
to give aunty a surprise.
A red gum growing near the house
has a garden round its base.
Mae never told a single soul
it was Freddy's resting place.

Strike Breaker

While sitting in a gondola
on the last night of their trip,
she really wasn't happy
and was giving him some lip.

So this is it. I'm not impressed.
You promised me romance.
There'd be champagne, flowers and chocolates,
lively music when we dance.

That's what you said, and silly me,
I believed your every word.
A romantic trip to Venice –
that's exactly what I heard.

And you wooed me with the promise of
a lovely gondola ride.
We'll cuddle up and drink champagne
as we'd very gently glide.

Tell me, why are we still waiting?
We've not moved a single inch.
And this worn-out seat my bum's on
is starting to really pinch.

The gondoliers are all on strike!
So that's why we're stuck here.
Then tell me why they let us on.
They should have made it clear.

We could be here for hours and hours.
It's our last night in this place.
I think we should point out to them
that we think it's a disgrace.

Well, I'm just not accepting it.
That is it! I'm getting off.
You're getting off, what do you mean?
I mean, I am getting off.

No! Do not stand up, *senora,*
the gondolier began to shout.
The canal is deep. If you fall in,
we canna pull you out.

But she was quite determined
and stepped out of the boat.
She sank beneath the water
but, alas, she didn't float.

The gondoliers were horrified,
but soon got on their way.
They still talk about the tragedy
that broke the strike that day.

DIY and a Husband Too

There was trouble in the household.
It just started with a drip.
She said, The basement floor is wet
and I'm scared that I might slip.

We had better call a plumber,
we've a leaking tap, she said.
No need for that – I'll fix it.
His words filled her with pure dread.
So off he set to the basement
with a hammer and a wrench.
I'll have it fixed in no time, love.
She felt her body clench.

He toiled away for several hours.
She knew something would go wrong.
Whatever is he doing there?
That has taken him so long.

Then suddenly, a mighty bang
resounded from below.
And water gushed from every tap –
she couldn't stop the flow.
She hurried to the cellar door.
Are you all right down there? she said.
Not a single word came back to her
so she wondered, was he dead?

Then from the cellar came his voice,
very shaky, not too clear.
I'm quite okay, a little wet.
Could you call the plumber, dear?

Dressing Room Danger

Can you help me with my zipper?
He was really quite distressed.
I got my tie caught in it
while rushing to get dressed.

The shop assistant tried to help
but didn't have much luck.
No matter how she pulled and strained,
the zip was firmly stuck.

She said, I'll get some lubricant
and we'll give the zip a spray.
Just try to get your trousers off.
But I've no undies on today!

I'll be naked from the waist, he said.
I will be out and floating free.
No problem. Please don't worry, sir,
that's nothing new for me to see.

He took his tie from round his neck,
worked his trousers to the floor.
Then stood there in his socks and shoes,
his shirt, and nothing more.

And then he heard a woman scream.
She stood at the unlocked door.
She'd come to use the dressing room,
not prepared for what she saw.

Help, help, she cried. A naked man
has exposed himself to me.
Several other people joined her
to see what there was to see.

He quickly shut and locked the door,
put his pants on in a flash.
And, tie still hanging from his zip,
he made a frantic dash.

When he reached his home to safety,
his wife said, How did you go?
Did you manage to get a new suit?
He said, The answer's no!

And, another thing, I am never
going back to that bloody store.
I do not need a brand-new suit,
I have told you that before.

And something else you need to know:
If I ever feel inclined
to go out without my undies,
you will know I've lost my mind.

Hair Raising

There, there, he said. It's not that bad.
Not bad! What is wrong with you?
You've botched the job, my hair is green.
Now what am I going to do?

I can't go out with bright, green hair,
you will have to fix this mess.
Well, not sure that I can fix it,
but I'll try and do my best.

You'll try your best! You'll try your best!
Excuse me, what do you mean?
When I walk out from here today,
my hair better not be green.

And if I lose a single strand
of my precious flowing mane,
I will sue your fancy arse off
and you'll never work again.

And think of the other clients
who have their hair done by you.
They're going to get an awful shock
when you're gone. What will they do?

For goodness sake, no need to fuss.
I am sure all will be well.
Just think of the funny story
you now will have to tell.

I know you're cross, but just calm down.
Didn't I warn you not to come?
The reason I said I'd do your hair
is because you are my mum.

Eye Opener

It was their grandson's exhibition
at the city gallery.
Always painting as a youngster,
now a man of twenty-three.

He'd developed as an artist,
and becoming quite renowned.
So, to see his exhibition,
Gramps and Gran had come to town.

Doors were unlocked very promptly
at the scheduled opening time.
Their grandson came towards them.
Come, I'll show you which is mine.

He took them to one painting
hanging on the gallery wall.
They followed close behind him,
then their smiles began to fall.

What the hell is that? Gramps whispered.
It's like someone's had a fit.
I think this painting's awful.
Do you think he ought to quit?

Hush, don't talk so loud. He'll hear you,
just make out you think it's grand.
What's wrong with you? her husband said.
This is light years short of grand.

It's messy and confusing,
what's it supposed to represent?
All that money paid for art school,
I wonder where it went.

Their grandson then spoke up and said,
I'm so very glad you're here.
This painting's in an abstract style –
it's a painting of a deer.

At this, Gramps made a gurgling sound.
Gran was scared he might pass out.
Is Gramps okay? her grandson asked.
Yes dear, it's just his gout.

Your painting is just wonderful,
it's so colourful and bright.
We're happy you invited us
to enjoy your special night.

Then Gramps, trying to be supportive,
said, My boy, you have done well.
Do you think the folks will like it?
Do you think it's going to sell?

I sold it for a fortune, Gramps,
said their grandson with a smile.
So I've booked that trip you wanted,
travelling Egypt and the Nile.

Missing in Action

He'd become quite slack and boring,
overweight, with smelly feet.
He would sit and watch the telly
drinking beer, then fall asleep.

She was upset, stressed and angry
that her husband didn't care.
He would rarely have a shower,
hardly ever comb his hair.

Why don't you warm things up a bit?
was a trusted friend's advice.
Your love life can be better
if you add a little spice.

So she went and bought a nightie
and some sexy underwear,
then she splashed herself with perfume.
But he didn't seem to care.

So, as a very last resort,
she devised a desperate plan.
If this won't fix him, nothing will –
I'll give up on this old man.

And then, at last, her world was changed.
She laughed with new-found glee.
What did she do? You well may ask.
She put Viagra in his tea.

Coffee and Conversation

They met at the local coffee shop
each Friday after lunch.
The three were in their eighties
and were such a happy bunch.
Their meetings were a ritual.
They would never miss a meet.
For their age group they were really fit
and quite steady on their feet.

A book group was enjoyed by Jack.
Playing golf savoured by Ted.
George really liked his dancing –
things that got them out of bed.
They enjoyed each other's stories
while they sipped their caffeine brew.
Getting together for chats
was what they loved to do.

One day when Jack, a little late,
looked sad – his mood was blue.
His friends were quite concerned and said,
Hey Jack, what's wrong with you?

I got kicked out of the book club.
They just sent me on my way,
and it really has upset me,
even more than I can say.
It was my turn to choose a book
so I really took my time
to pick one that would excite,
and I thought my choice was fine.

According to the book club group,
my selection was depraved.
And as a group they wondered,
Was I stupid or just brave?

His friends were now quite curious.
Jack, whatever did you choose?
A book brimful of pictures.
I thought I couldn't lose.
But sadly, now I have to go.
In the book club I've no future.
The book I chose – they didn't like –
was called the *Karma Sutra*.

The Big Question

He was quietly contented,
curled up in his favourite chair.
There was nothing to disturb him
until she was standing there.

She'd been busy in the bedroom
trying on a brand-new dress.
They were going to a party
and she wanted to impress.

My bum, does it look big in this?
He pretended not to hear.
Are you listening to me, husband?
He looked up and said, Yes, dear.

Well, I'm asking your opinion.
I can't quite make up my mind.
Then she turned her back towards him,
and her bum to him inclined.

He knew he couldn't lie to her.
He would have to tell the truth.
So he took a very careful look
and then he called out, Strewth!

It was then he saw the price tag.
So he went on the attack:
Yes, your bum looks very big in this.
I suggest you take it back.

Faith Can Move Mountains

I think I'm in decline, said Tom.
Why is that? his good wife said.
Well, nothing's really working,
I might as well be dead.

My eyesight's dim, my teeth are gone,
my legs are week and shaky,
and the skin upon my body
is thin and pale and flaky.

We're very old and that's not fun,
said his sweet devoted wife.
But, my darling, we're still breathing
and can still enjoy our life.

Shall we go and see the preacher
who is saying he can heal?
I don't believe that crap, he said,
we both know that can't be real.

Well, let's go and have a listen
and see what he's all about.
Even if we don't believe him,
it could be a fun day out.

The preacher man soon drew them in
with his message strong and clear.
Dear friends, said he, if you have faith,
there will be healing here.

Now with your hand, the preacher said,
just very gently touch
the place where you need healing.
Tom placed his on his crotch.

She put her hand upon her knee,
then smiled at Tom's selection.
My darling, he said 'healing'.
He did not say 'resurrection'.

A Letter from Mum

My darling son

Put your clean clothes in the wardrobe,
don't leave them on the floor.
It's really not that hard a task,
that is what the wardrobe's for.

Don't get me wrong, we love you
and we know you try your best.
You're twenty-one, the time has come
to leave this cosy nest.

We've decided to release you
and send you on your way.
You might find a job, earn money.
I am sure you'll be okay.

No, I mustn't try to stop you
and keep you close to me.
It isn't fair, the world's out there.
Go through the door, be free.

We will not change our mind on this
no matter what you say.
We've loaded up the caravan
and we're rolling out today.

The Choice

I have to make a choice, said Fred.
It's between Marjorie and May.
I have been dating both of them
and they're great in their own way.

But as they're a little younger,
each of them just eighty-three,
it is really hard to please them
when they both want sex with me.

Why do you have to make a choice?
inquired his drinking mate.
Well, dating both has worn me out –
an early death could be my fate.

His mate was really quite amazed
that, at the age of ninety-one,
his friend still had the stamina
to have two women on the run.

The trouble is that neither knows
the other one exists.
So it can be very tricky
setting up my little trysts.

I don't know if it's worth it,
all this cloak-and-dagger stuff.
After I visit both of them,
I am really out of puff.

A few days later at the pub,
Fred appeared to be upset.
His mate was quite concerned and asked,
Have you made your hard choice yet?

Oh, it's been made all right, said Fred,
and it's one that's meant to be.
It seems the two of them found out
they had both been dating me.

When I went to see Marjorie,
May was waiting for me too.
When they both gave me the finger,
that was it, we three were through.

So, though it's sad, it now appears
Marj and May with me are done.
I think I'll join the bingo group
though I'll miss the naughty fun.

www.ingramcontent.com/pod-product-compliance
Lightning Source LLC
Chambersburg PA
CBHW071007080526
44587CB00015B/2378